DINGLE IN PICTURES

CORCA DHUIBHNE TRÍ SHÚILIBH AN CHEAMARA
DINGLE EN IMAGES
DINGLE IN BILDERN

Steve MacDonogh

To the memory of Anne Chapireau

Acknowledgements
My thanks go to the many people of the area who have contributed to my appreciation of the Dingle Peninsula, and to Máire, Siobhán, Deirdre, Cathal and Seán, who all helped with the selection of the slides.

A note on the photographs
All the photographs in this book were taken with an Olympus OM1n; in most cases the film used was Fuji Velvia.

First published in 2001 by Brandon,
an imprint of Mount Eagle Publications,
Sliabh an Fhiolair Teoranta, Dingle, Co. Kerry, Ireland.

All photographs and text © Steve MacDonogh 2001

The author has asserted his moral rights.

British Library Cataloguing in Publication Data
is available for this book.

ISBN 0 86322 279 X

Design and typesetting: Bright Idea, Killarney

Printed by CraftPrint

I gcuimhne ar Anne Chapireau

Buíochas
Gabhaim buíochas le gach duine a chabhraigh liom tuiscint a fháil ar leithinis Chorca Dhuibhne, agus le Máire, Siobhán, Deirdre, Cathal agus Seán, a chabhraigh liom na sleamhnáin a roghnú.

Na pictiúirí
Tógadh na pictiúirí ar fad sa leabhar seo le Olympus OM1n; is ar scannán Fuji Velvia is mó a tógadh iad seo.

Foilsithe den chéad uair i 2001 ag Brandon,
inphrionta le Mount Eagle Publications,
Sliabh an Fhiolair Teoranta,
Daingean Uí Chúise, Co. Chiarraí, Éire.

Pictiúirí agus téacs © Steve MacDonogh 2001

ISBN 0 86322 279 X

Dearadh agus Clóchur: Bright Idea, Cill Airne

Priontáil: CraftPrint

En souvenir d'Anne Chapireau

Remerciements
Je tiens à adresser mes vifs remerciements aux habitants de la péninsule de Dingle qui m'ont aidé à m'imprégner de l'âme de ce lieu, sans oublier Máire, Siobhán, Deirdre, Cathal et Séan pour leur contribution lors de la sélection des photos.

Remarques sur les photos
Les photos publiées dans ce livre ont été prises avec un Olympus OM1n et, le plus souvent, avec un film Fuji Velvia.

Première édition publiée par Brandon
Marque d'éditeur: Mount Eagle Publications,
Sliabh an Fhiolair Teoranta,
Dingle, Co. Kerry, Irlande, 2001.

© Steve MacDonogh 2001 pour le texte et les photos

ISBN 0 86322 279 X

Tous droits réservés.

Composition et conception graphique: Bright Idea, Killarney

Imprimé sur les presses de la société CraftPrint

Zur Erinnerung an Anne Chapireau

Danksagungen
Ich möchte mich bei all denjenigen Menschen bedanken, die zu meinem Verständnis und meiner Wertschätzung der Dingle-Halbinsel beigetragen haben, und bei Máire, Siobhán, Deirdre, Cathal und Sean, die mir bei der Auswahl der Dias geholfen haben.

Anmerkung zu den Fotografien
Alle Fotos in diesem Buch wurden mit einer Olympus OM1n aufgenommen; in den meisten Fällen wurde ein Fuji Velvia Film benutzt.

Originalausgabe erschien 2001 bei Brandon,
eine Lizenzausgabe mit Genehmigung des Mount Eagle Verlages, Sliabh an Fhiolair Teoranta, Dingle, Co. Kerry, Ireland.

Alle Fotografien und Text © Steve MacDonogh 2001

ISBN 0 86322 279 X

Design und Satz: Bright Idea, Killarney

Druck: CraftPrint

The Dingle peninsula was described in *The National Geographic Traveler* as "the most beautiful place on earth", and in David Lean's film *Ryan's Daughter* it was perhaps the scenery of this south-western tip of Europe that impressed viewers the most. Bounded on three sides by the sea, it enjoys a slightly milder climate than its neighbouring mainland, causing many plants to flourish exceptionally well - most notably the fuchsia with its deep red flowers against dark green leaves. The peninsula combines in its landscape the rugged coastal scenery of rocky outcrops and cliffs with the soft shapes of hills and mountains, skirted by green lowlands and long stretches of sandy beaches.

There is a depth in the appeal of the landscape which goes beyond the contemplation of beautiful scenery, for the countryside is dotted with historical remains and artefacts. The Dingle peninsula possesses a quite extraordinary concentration of archaeological sites. These testify physically to the rich culture of the past, and the peninsula is also an exceptionally rich repository of folklore and of Irish traditional culture. Today in the area to the west of Dingle town Irish is very much the first language; traditional music and dance play an important part in many people's lives, and small boats of ancient design are still built and used.

Inevitably, the visitor's response to Dingle is an individual one. Many visit for the contact with Irish spoken in a natural, native way; others visit because it is a kind of paradise for the walker; others to observe the flora and fauna. For many the atmosphere of simply being there, of impromptu meetings or musical sessions in pubs, is like a restoring breath of fresh air to which they will wish constantly to return.

There must be few for whom the surrounding presence of the sea does not provide abiding images. I have tried to capture this presence in my photographs, but to capture also what is often less seen: the contrast between a lush tree-lined field of yellow irises and an empty expanse of bog only a few miles away; the silent valleys that lie off the beaten track; the customs of the place, from holy wells to the Dingle Races.

"An áit is áille ar domhan". Mar seo a chuir *The National Geographic Traveler* síos ar leithinis Chorca Dhuibhne, agus níl aon dabht ná gurb iad na radharcanna agus an tírdhreach is mó a chuaigh i bhfeidhm ar dhaoine sa scannán cáiliúil *Ryan's Daughter* le David Lean.

Tá aeráid Chorca Dhuibhne beagán níos boige ná mar atá níos faide isteach fén dtír de bharr go bhfuil an fharraige ar thrí thaobh de agus bíonn borradh dá réir faoin bhfásra, go háirithe an fiúise nó deora Dé leis na bláthanna dorcha dearg agus na duilleoga glasa.

Ach tá a thuilleadh fós le feiscint. Tá iarsmaí cianársa seandálaíochta scaipthe go forleathan ar fuaid na leithinise. Anseo a gheobhair fíor-chultúr na hÉireann, saibhreas teanga agus béaloidis i ngach aon bhall. Gaelainn is mó a labhartar laistiar de Dhaingean, agus maireann traidisiún an cheoil agus an rince go láidir. Sa lá inniu féin bíonn báid de dhéantús ársa - na naomhóga - á dtógaint agus á n-úsáid.

Gan dabht, tugann daoine turas ar an nDaingean ar chúiseann difriúla. Tagann go leor daoine chun an Ghaelainn a chlos á labhairt i measc na ndaoine, tagann a thuilleadh ar thóir na siúlóidí breátha atá ar fuaid na leithinise, agus tagann a thuilleadh fós ar mhaithe leis an gceol agus leis an gcraic. Nuair a chuireann daoine aithne ar an gceantar, is breá leo filleadh arís is arís.

Téann an fharraige i bhfeidhm ar chách. Dá réir sin, tá go leor pictiúirí den bhfarraige sa chnuasach seo agam. Ach tá pictiúirí suaithinseacha eile ann chomh maith, pictiúirí a thabharfaidh léargas eile ar áilleacht na dúthaí - na bláthanna, na portaigh, nósanna na háite, na toibreacha beannaithe agus fiú Ráiseanna an Daingin.

Selon le *National Geographic Traveler*, la péninsule de Dingle est «le plus bel endroit au monde». Dans le film de David Lean, *Ryan's Daughter*, les spectateurs ont été avant tout enthousiasmés par les paysages de cette pointe du sud-ouest de l'Europe. Grâce à la proximité de la mer, la région bénéficie d'un climat plus doux que l'intérieur des terres, favorisant ainsi la floraison exceptionnelle de nombreuses plantes locales - notamment celle du fuchsia dont les fleurs écarlates contrastent avec le vert profond de ses feuilles. Ces paysages sont une association harmonieuse de collines aux pentes douces et de rivages rocailleux et déchiquetés, entrelacés de prés verts et de plages de sable.

La force de l'attrait exercé par le paysage va au-delà des vues superbes qu'il offre: la campagne est truffée de vestiges de peuples anciens, d'objets chargés d'histoire et sa concentration en sites archéologiques est impressionnante. Le folklore et la culture traditionnelle irlandaises sont des caractéristiques essentielles de la péninsule, témoins vivants d'une riche culture ancestrale. Aujourd'hui encore, l'irlandais est la langue dominante de la région située à l'ouest de la ville de Dingle. Les anciens petits bateaux y sont toujours construits et utilisés et la danse et la musique irlandaises jouent un rôle prépondérant dans la vie de ses habitants.

Chaque visiteur trouve ici son compte. Beaucoup de gens y viennent pour pratiquer la langue irlandaise dans son contexte, d'autres pour profiter de ce que l'on peut à juste titre appeler le paradis du randonneur, d'autres encore pour étudier la faune et la flore locales. Le simple fait de se trouver là, l'imprévisibilité des rencontres et les manifestations musicales dans les pubs sont comme une bouffée d'oxygène qui donnera incessamment à chacun envie de revenir.

A quelques rares exceptions près, l'omniprésence de l'océan imprime dans les esprits des images indélébiles. Dans mes photographies, j'ai voulu rendre cette présence mais aussi saisir ce qui est plus difficilement perceptible: le contraste entre un champ luxuriant d'iris des marais bordé d'arbres et une tourbière désertique située à quelques kilomètres de là, les vallées silencieuses qui s'étendent loin des sentiers battus ou encore les symboles du lieu, allant des fontaines miraculeuses aux courses de Dingle.

Die Zeitschrift *The National Geographic Traveler* beschrieb die Dingle-Halbinsel als "den schönsten Ort der Welt", und in David Leans Film *Ryan's Daughter* war es vielleicht die Landschaft dieser südwestlichsten Spitze Europas, die die Kinobesucher am meisten beeindruckt hat.

Das Meer, das die Halbinsel von drei Seiten umschliesst, verleiht der Gegend ein etwas milderes Klima als das des angrenzenden Binnenlandes, was zur Folge hat, dass viele Pflanzen dort besonders gut gedeihen - am auffälligsten unter ihnen ist die Fuchsie mit ihren tiefroten Blüten und dunkelgrünen Blättern. Die landschaftliche Vielfalt der Halbinsel beherbergt zerklüftete Felsklippen neben sanften Hügelketten und Berglandschaften, grüne Niederungen und weitläufige Sandstrände.

Ein tieferer Reiz dieser Landschaft, weitaus mehr als eine blosse Betrachtung der Naturschönheiten, liegt verborgen in den historischen Überresten und Artefakten, die über die ganze Gegend verstreut liegen. Die Dingle-Halbinsel besitzt eine ausserordentliche Ansammlung archäologischer Stätten, die Zeugnis einer vielfaltigen Kultur früherer Zeiten ablegen, und verfügt zudem über eine reichhaltige Quelle von Folklore und traditioneller, irischer Kultur. Immer noch ist Gälisch die vorherrschende Sprache westlich der Stadt Dingle; traditionelle Musik und Tanz spielen eine wichtige Rolle im Leben der Einwohner, und kleine Fischerboote uralten Designs werden heute noch gebaut und benutzt.

Zweifellos wird Dingle auf jeden Besucher einen individuellen Eindruck machen. Viele besuchen die Halbinsel, um die gälische Sprache in ihrem natürlichen und ursprünglichen Kontext zu erfahren; andere, weil sie eine Art von Paradies für Bergwanderer ist; wiederum andere aus Interesse an der speziellen Flora und Fauna. Für viele Besucher ist es ganz einfach die erfrischende Erfahrung eines unmittelbaren Lebensstils, unerwartete Begegnungen oder improvisierte Musiksessions, die sie immer wieder dorthin zurückziehen.

Es dürfte nur wenige unter ihnen geben, denen die stete Gegenwart des Meeres keine bleibende Erinnerung hinterlässt. Ich habe versucht, diese Gegenwart in meinen Fotografien einzufangen, aber auch das, was auf den ersten Blick weniger ersichtlich ist: den Kontrast von sattgrünen, von Bäumen gesäumten Feldern voller gelber Schwertlilien und ausladenden Flächen kahlen Hochmoors; die stillen, abgelegenen Täler; die Sitten und Gebräuche der Gegend, von heiligen Brunnen bis zu den Pferderennen von Dingle.

Steve MacDonogh is the author of *The Dingle Peninsula*, which has been described as "far and away the best of the many books written about the area" (*Irish Examiner*). A publisher, poet, local historian and folklorist, he is also the author of *Green and Gold: The Wrenboys of Dingle* and *By Dingle Bay and Blasket Sound*; his publishing autobiography, *Open Book: One Publisher's War* was published in 1999.

Steve MacDonogh est l'auteur de *The Dingle Peninsula*: l'*Irish Examiner* considère qu'il s'agit là «de loin du meilleur ouvrage parmi les nombreux livres écrits sur la région». Editeur, poète, historien local et folkloriste, il est aussi l'auteur de *Green and Gold: The Wrenboys of Dingle* et *By Dingle Bay and Blasket Sound*. Son autobiographie, *Open Book: One Publisher's War*, a été publiée en 1999.

Dúradh an *Irish Examiner* gurb é *The Dingle Peninsula* le Steve MacDonogh "an leabhar is fearr dár scríobhadh faoi Chorca Dhuibhne". I measc na leabhar eile a scríobh sé tá *Green and Gold: The Wrenboys of Dingle* agus *By Dingle Bay and Blasket Sound*. Foilsíodh leabhar leis faoin chuid foilsitheoireachta, *Open Book: One Publisher's War* sa bhliain 1999. Foilsitheoir, údar, file, staraí áitiúil agus béaloideasóir is ea é.

Steve MacDonogh ist der Autor von *The Dingle Peninsula*, einem Buch, das die irische Tageszeitung *The Irish Examiner* als "das bei weitem beste der vielen Bücher über diese Gegend" beschrieben hat. Er ist als Verleger tätig, ist Dichter, Historiker in Heimatkunde und Folklorist und hat ausserdem *Green and Gold: The Wrenboys of Dingle* und *By Dingle Bay and Blasket Sound* veröffentlicht. Seine Autobiografie über seine Tätigkeit als Verleger *One Publisher's War* wurde 1999 veröffentlicht.

The Great Blasket island, rising like a great whale from the treacherous sea at the south-western end of the Dingle peninsula, was home to a remarkable community of people, whose stories are told in a succession of books - most notably *An tOileánach/ The Islandman* (1929) by Tomás Ó Criomhthain, *Fiche Bliain ag Fás/Twenty Years A-Growing* (1933) by Muiris Ó Suilleabháin and *Peig* (1936) by Peig Sayers.

An Blascaod Mór ag éirí go maorga as an bhfarraige ag cúinne thiar theas na leithinse. Mhair pobal daoine ar an oileán agus tá cur síos déanta ar an saol seo sna leabhra cáiliúla *An tOileánach/The Islandman* (1929) le Tomás Ó Criomhthain, *Fiche Bliain ag Fás/Twenty Years A-Growing* (1933) le Muiris Ó Súilleabháin agus *Peig* (1936) le Peig Sayers.

L'île de Great Blasket, à l'image de la grande baleine, semble jaillir hors des flots entourant la péninsule de Dingle. Elle fut le foyer d'une remarquable communauté d'individus, dont l'histoire nous est contée dans de nombreux livres. Les plus connus sont *An tOileánach/The Islandman* (1929) de Tomás Ó Criomhthain, *Fiche Bliain ag Fás/Twenty Years A-Growing* (1933) de Muiris Ó Suilleabháin et *Peig* (1936) de Peig Sayers.

Die Great Blasket Insel, die, einem riesigen Wal gleich, in den gefährlichen Meeresströmungen vor der Südwestspitze der Dingle-Halbinsel liegt, war einst die Heimat einer bemerkenswerten Einwohnergemeinde, deren Geschichten in einer Reihe von Büchern erhalten geblieben sind, allen voran *An tOileánach/The Islandman* (1926) von Tomás Ó Criomhthain, *Fiche Bliain ag Fás/Twenty Years A-Growing* (1933) von Muiris Ó Suilleabháin und *Peig* (1936) von Peig Sayers.

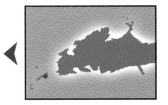

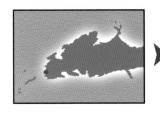

The Blasket ferry arrives in Dunquin. The island was evacuated in the early 1950s, but it is much visited in the summer months.

Bád farantóireachta ón mBlascaod ag teacht isteach ar ché Dhún Chaoin. Aistríodh na daoine amach ar an míntír sna caogadaí, ach tugann go leor cuairteoirí turas ar an oileán sa tsamhradh.

Arrivée du ferry de Blasket à Dunquin, île désertée au début des années 1950 mais très visitée pendant les mois d'été.

Die Blasketfähre legt in Dunquin an. Die Insel wurde Anfang der 50ger Jahre evakuiert, wird aber heute während der Sommermonate regelmässsig von Einheimischen und Touristen besucht.

▼ Clogher strand in the light of a winter evening.

▼ Tráigh Chloichir, tráthnóna geimhridh.

▼ Clogher strand à la lumière d'un soir d'hiver.

▼ Der Strand von Clogher im winterlichen Abendlicht.

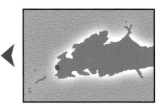

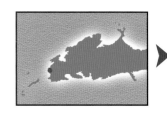

▶ Clogher strand in rough weather, with Inishtooskert.

▶ Tráigh Chloichir agus Inis Tuaisceart le linn stoirme.

▶ Tempête sur Clogher strand et Inishtooskert.

▶ Der Strand von Clogher bei stürmischem Wetter, mit Inishtooskert.

▼ Coumeenole and Dunmore Head, with the Great Blasket obscured by the low cloud of a summer morning.

▼ Coumeenole et Dunmore head: matin d'été à Great Blasket assombri par un nuage bas.

▼ Com Dhíneol agus an Dún Mór, is an tOileán faoi bhrat scamaill maidin shamhraidh.

▼ Coumeenole und Dunmore Head mit der von den tiefhängenden Wolken eines Sommermorgen verdeckten Great Blasket Island.

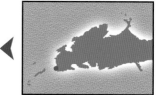

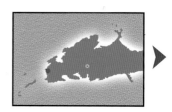

► Clogher and the Three Sisters

► Clogher et les Three Sisters.

► Cloichear agus na Triúr Deirféar.

► Clogher und die Three Sisters.

▼ Coumeenole: the waters around the Dingle peninsula offer superb conditions for surfers and windsurfers.

▼ Com Dhíneol. Tá na farraigí timpeall ar leithinis Chorca Dhuibhne an-oiriúnach do dhaoine gur maith leo clárseoltóireacht.

▼ Coumeenole: les eaux baignant la péninsule de Dingle sont le paradis des surfeurs et des véliplanchistes.

▼ Coumeenole: die Gewässer um die Dingle-Halbinsel bieten hervorragende Bedingungen fur Surfer und Windsurfer.

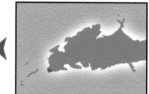

▶ Coumeenole beach, a popular spot on a fine summer's day, and scene of action in David Lean's film, *Ryan's Daughter*.

▶ Tráigh Chom Dhíneol. Bíonn an tráigh seo lán go maith sa tsamhradh agus is anseo a tógadh cuid de na radharcanna sa scannán *Ryan's Daughter* le David Lean.

▶ Plage de Coumeenole, très appréciée pendant les beaux jours d'été et lieu de tournage de l'une des scènes du film de David Lean: *Ryan's Daughter*.

▶ Der Strand von Coumeenole, ein beliebter Ort an schönen Sommertagen und Drehort von David Leans Film *Ryan's Daughter*.

On the day of the Blessing of the Boats the Dingle fleet heads out from the pier to the harbour's mouth. This annual festival celebrates the importance of fishing in the life of the town.

Beannú na mBád sa Daingean. Ceiliúradh mór é seo a tharlaíonn uair sa mbliain, agus taispeánann sé an tábhacht atá le tionscail na hiascaireachta sa Daingean.

Jour de la bénédiction des bateaux: la flotte de Dingle quitte la jetée et se dirige vers l'entrée du port. Cette fête annuelle célèbre l'importance de la pêche dans la vie locale.

Am Tag der "Segnung der Boote" fährt die Fischereiflotte von Dingle vom Pier zur Hafeneinfahrt. Diese alljährliche Sitte feiert die Bedeutung der Fischerei im Leben der Stadt.

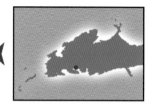

Blessing of the boats.

Beannú na mBád.

La bénédiction des bateaux.

Segnung der Boote.

▼ Boats at rest in the evening at Dingle harbour.

▼ Báid ceangailte le cé an Daingin.

▼ Bateaux amarrés dans le port de Dingle, le soir.

▼ Fischkutter am Pier im Abendlicht von Dingle.

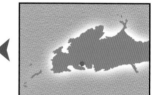

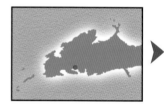

▶ Shop in Main Street, Dingle. Many shops flourished in Dingle before the onset of tourism, providing a commercial centre for a large swathe of the surrounding countryside.

▶ Siopa sa tSráid Mhór. Bhí go leor siopaí beaga sa Daingean sara dtosnaigh aon turasóireacht, agus bhí tarrac mhuintir na dúthaí ar fad orthu.

▶ Magasin dans Main Street à Dingle. De nombreux magasins sont apparus avant l'arrivée du tourisme, conférant une vie commerciale à une grande partie de la campagne avoisinante.

▶ Laden in Main Street, Dingle. Viele Geschäte florierten auch vor Beginn des Fremdenverkehrs in Dingle, da es als Geschäftszentrum für die umliegenden, ländlichen Gebiete diente.

▼ Dingle shopfronts, Strand Street.

▼ Siopaí ar Bhóthar na Trá.

▼ Devantures de magasins dans Strand Street à Dingle.

▼ Ladenfassaden von Dingle, Strand Street.

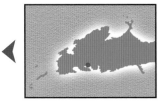

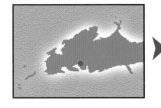

▶ The Dingle Races, held annually in August, provide one of the most lively and colourful weekends of the year. A "flapper" meeting, it attracts horses, their owners and riders from all over Ireland, and some from across the Irish Sea.

▶ Ceann de na deireadh seachtainí móra sa bhliain is ea Ráiseanna an Daingin. Tagann lucht na gcapall isteach 'on Daingean ó gach cúinne den dtír agus fiú amháin thar lear.

▶ Les courses de Dingle qui se déroulent chaque année au mois d'août représentent l'une des manifestations les plus colorées et vivantes de l'année. Une rencontre appelée «flapper»: de nombreux chevaux, cavaliers et propriétaires de chevaux venus de toute l'Irlande et d'autres pays y participent.

▶ Die Pferderennen in Dingle, die jedes Jahr im August stattfinden, bieten eines der lebhaftesten und farbenfrohesten Wochenenden des Jahres. Zum "flapper meeting" (ein Treffen ausserhalb des Rennverbandes) finden sich Pferde, ihre Besitzer und Jockeys aus ganz Irland ein, sowie auch aus Grossbritannien.

▼ Dingle town from Greenmount.

▼ Baile an Daingin ón gCnoicín.

▼ Dingle depuis Greenmount.

▼ Blick auf Dingle von Greenmount.

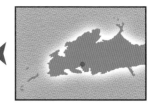

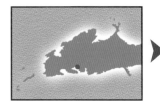

▶ On St Stephen's Day, 26 December, groups of Dingle's citizens dress in suits of straw and other disguises; carrying banners and preceded by hobby horses, they parade the town with bands of fife (or tin whistle) and drum. Here in Dingle this unbroken tradition celebrates a custom which was once part of a European-wide mid-winter festival.

▶ Lá an Dreoilín, an 26ú Nollaig, sa Daingean. Siúlann na Dreoilíní sráideanna an Daingin ag seinm cheoil le drumaí agus fífeanna, iad feistithe go suaithinseach don ócáid.

▶ Le 26 Décembre, jour de la Saint Stéphane, les habitants de la ville de Dingle se déguisent en revêtant, par example, des costumes de paille, paradent dans la ville, portant des bannières et des effigies de chevaux au rythme des joueurs de fifre et de tambour. Cette tradition, toujours vivante, est l'une des coutumes du festival mi-hivernal célébré autrefois dans toute l'Europe.

▶ Am Tag des Heiligen Stephan, dem 26. Dezember, verkleiden sich verschiedene Gruppen der Einwohner von Dingle in Strohkostümen und anderen Vermummungen. Angeführt von Bannerträgern und grossen Steckenpferden ziehen sie durch die Strassen, gefolgt von einer Band mit Querflöten (oder Blechflöten) und Trommeln. Diese ungebrochene Tradition führt einen Brauch fort, der einst Teil eines europaweiten Mitwinterfestes war.

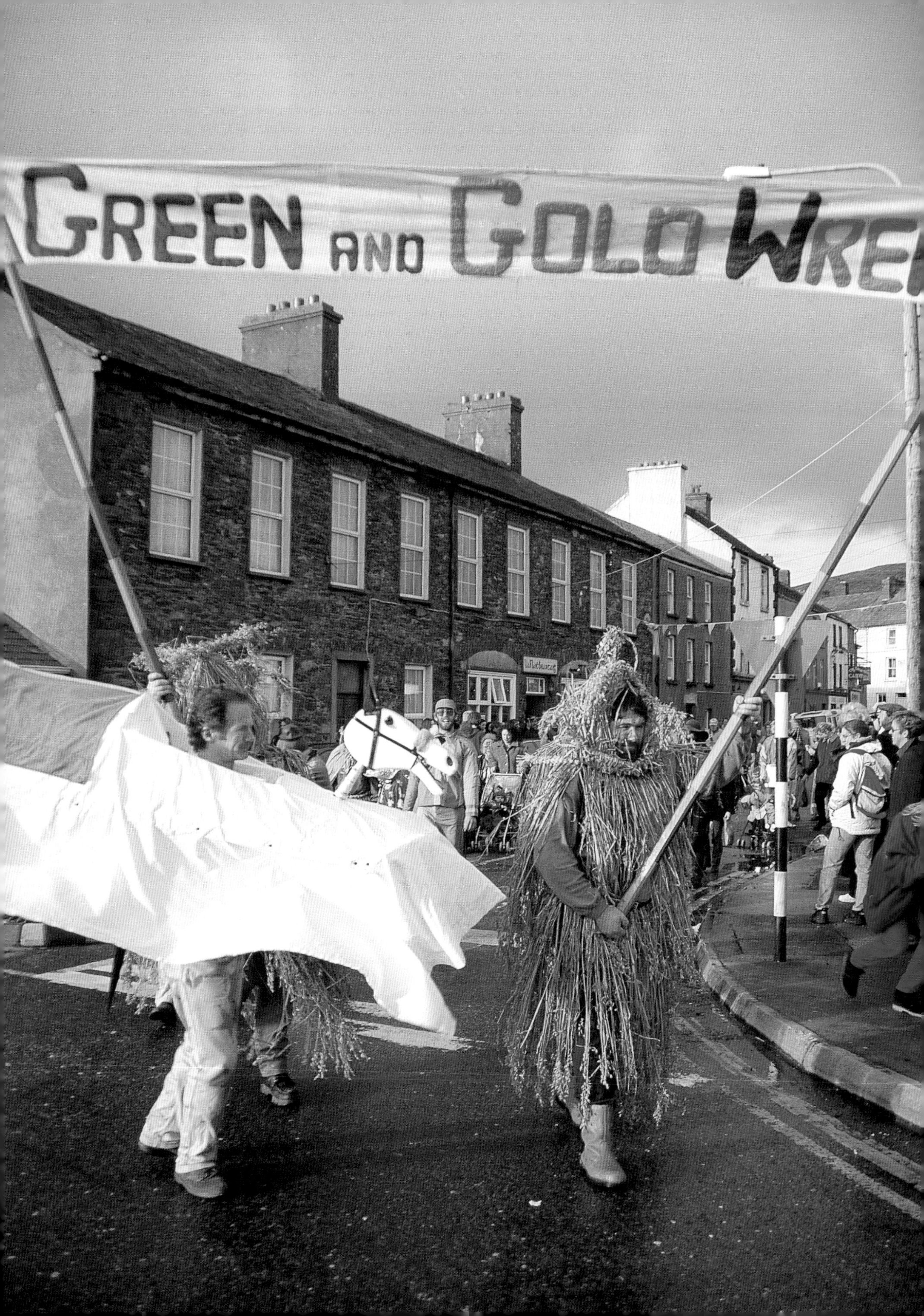
GREEN AND GOLD

▼ Burnham: looking from the lagoon towards Dingle harbour.

▼ Baile an Ghóilín: radharc ar chuan an Daingin.

▼ Burnham: vue du lagon en direction du port de Dingle.

▼ Burnham: Blick von der Lagune auf den Hafen von Dingle.

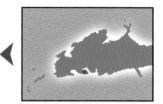

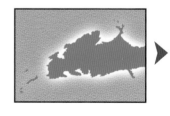

▶ Fuchsia, a native of Argentina and common in New Zealand, was introduced to the Dingle peninsula early in the twentieth century; it prospered in the warm and wet conditions and is now a beautiful feature of the scenery.

▶ Tugadh an fiúise isteach go Corca Dhuibhne go luath sa bhfichiú haois. Is í an Airgintín tír dhúchais an phlanda seo agus fásann sé go forleathan sa Nua-Shéalainn chomh maith. Oireann aeráid bhogthais Chorca Dhuibhne go maith dó agus tá sé ar cheann de na radharcanna is deise ar fuaid na leithinise.

▶ Fuchsia. Originaire d'Argentine et très répandu en Nouvelle-Zélande, le fuchsia fit son apparition sur la péninsule de Dingle au cours du vingtième siècle. Le climat doux et humide lui a permis de prospérer et il donne aujourd'hui au paysage une touche haute en couleur.

▶ Die Fuchsie, eine in Argentinien beheimatete Pflanze, weit verbreitet auch in Neuseeland, wurde im frühen 20. Jahrhundert auf die Dingle-Halbinsel eingeführt. Sie verbreitete sich schnell in dem feuchten und warmen Klima und säumt heute fast alle Landstrassen der Halbinsel.

The early Chistian oratory of Teampall Mhanachain (St Manchan's church), which is also known as Teampall Geall (the white or bright church).

Aireagal Mhancháin ó luathré na Críostaíochta. Glaotar an Teampall Geal air chomh maith.

L'oratoire de Teampall Mhanachain (église de St Manchan), datant du début de l'ère chrétienne est également connu sous le nom de Teampall Geall (l'église lumineuse).

Das frühchristliche Oratorium Teampall Mhanachain (St Manchans Kapelle), auch bekannt unter dem Namen Teampeall Geall (die weisse oder helle Kapelle).

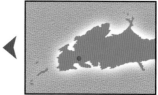

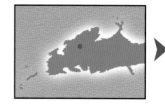

A now-deserted valley which was once occupied and farmed, Coumaloghig is approached across this ford.

An t-áth go Com an Lochaigh. Tá an baile seo tréigthe anois ach mhair pobal daoine ann tráth.

Une vallée aujourd'hui désertée mais autrefois habitée et cultivée: elle permet d'accéder à Coumaloghig.

Coumaloghig, ein heute verlassenes Tal, das früher bewohnt und bewirtschaftet war, wird über diese Furt erreicht.

▼ A ruined house at Kilvickadownig.

▼ Fothrach tí i gCill Mhic an Domhnaigh.

▼ Maison en ruines de Kilvickadownig.

▼ Eine Ruine in Kilvickadownig.

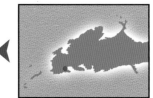

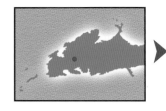

▶ The gallán at Lateevemanagh is the tallest standing stone in the Dingle peninsula, and stands 4.75 metres high.

▶ Is é an gallán seo i Leataoibh Meánach an ceann is aoirde ar an leithinis. Tá sé 4.75 méadar ar aoirde.

▶ Le gallán de Lateevemanagh, d'une hauteur de 4,75 mètres, est le plus grand menhir de la péninsule de Dingle.

▶ Der "gallan" in Lateevemanagh ist der grössste stehende Stein auf der Dingle-Halbinsel, mit einer Höhe von 4,75 m.

▼ Looking towards Mount Brandon from the bridge at Feohanagh.

▼ Radharc ar Chnoc Bhréanainn ó dhroichead na Feothanaí.

▼ Vue du Mont Brandon depuis le pont de Feohanagh.

▼ Blick auf Mount Brandon von der Brücke in Feohanagh.

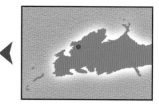

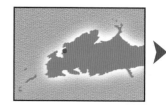

▶ The jagged western coastline of the peninsula from Dooneen pier.

▶ Cósta thiar na leithinise ó ché an Dúinín.

▶ Vue du littoral déchiqueté de la péninsule depuis la jetée de Dooneen.

▶ Die zerklüftete Westküste der Halbinsel beim Pier in Dooneen.

▼ The large early cross, the holed ogham stone, and the twelfth-century Romanesque church of Kilmalkedar, centre of the development of early Chistianity in the Dingle peninsula.

▼ Cros, cloch oghaim agus séipéal den stíl Rómhánúil ón dara haois déag i gCill Maolchéadair, lár-ionad thús na Críostaíochta i gCorca Dhuibhne.

▼ Majestueuse croix ancienne, la pierre Ogham perforée et l'église romane du douzième siècle de Kilmalkedar, lieu central du développement des débuts du christianisme sur la péninsule de Dingle.

▼ Das grosse, frühchristliche Steinkreuz, der Ogham-Stein und die romanische Kirche von Kilmalkedar aus dem 12. Jahrhundert, einst Mittelpunkt in der Entwicklung des frühen Christentums auf der Dingle-Halbinsel.

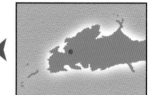
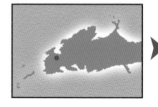

▶ The fine cross-slab at Reask, a Christian settlement of the fifth to seventh centuries.

▶ Cros ar an Riasc, láthair Chríostaí ón 5ú-7ú haois.

▶ Superbe pierre de Reask (pierre mégalithique sur laquelle est gravée une croix), peuplement chrétien du cinquième au septième siècle.

▶ Ein gutes Beispiel eines Steines mit eingemeisseltem Kreuz in Reask, einer frühchristlichen Siedlung aus dem 5. bis 7. Jahrhundert.

▼ The beach at Beal Bawn.

▼ Tráigh Bhéal Bán.

▼ Plage de Beal Bawn.

▼ Der Strand bei Beal Bawn.

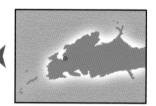

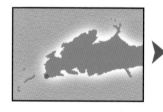

▶ Coumeenole

▶ Com Dhíneol

▶ Coumeenole

▶ Coumeenole

▼ Gallarus oratory, a perfect early building constructed by the method of dry-stone corbelling. Most such oratories were made in the seventh and eighth centuries, but this outstanding example may have been built a little later. There is a burial area beside the oratory with a seventh century cross-slab.

▼ Séipéilín Ghallarais. Tógadh formhór na séipéal dá leithéid seo sa 7ú nó sa 8ú haois, ach b'fhéidir gur tógadh an ceann iontach seo beagán níos déanaí. Tá láthair adhlactha mar a bhfuil cros ón 7ú haois in aice láimhe.

▼ L'oratoire de Gallarus, une construction typique réalisée selon la méthode de l'encorbellement de la pierre séchée. La plupart des oratoires de ce type furent construits aux 7ème et 8ème siècles mais celui-ci semble plus récent. Une sépulture marquée par une croix de pierre se trouve à côté de l'oratoire.

▼ Das Gallarus Oratorium, ein perfektes Beispiel der Kragsteinbauweise und des Mauerbaus ohne Mörtel. Die meisten solcher Oratorien wurden im 7. und 8. Jahrhundert erbaut, aber dieser aussergewöhnliche Bau kann etwas späteren Datums sein. Ausserhalb des Oratoriums befindet sich eine Begräbnisstätte mit einem Stein mit eingemeisseltem Kreuz aus dem 7. Jahrhundert.

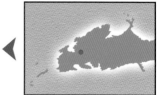

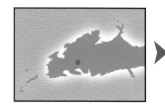

▶ The slender and elegant cross-slab at the early Christian settlement of Kilfountain; it bears a Greek cross and the name of the founder of the settlement, Finten.

▶ Ar láthair Chríostaí Chill Fhiontain: Tá an ainm Finten, an té a bhunaigh an láthair, agus cros Ghréagach gearrtha sa chloch.

▶ Croix de pierre particulièrement intéressante du peuplement de Kilfountain: elle date des débuts de la chrétienté, est ornée d'une croix grecque et mentionne le nom de Finten, fondateur de ce peuplement.

▶ Die schmale und elegante Steintafel mit eingemeisseltem, griechischen Kreuz in der frühchristlichen Siedlung in Kilfountain; der Stein trägt den Namen des Siedlungsgründers, Finten.

▼ Pinguicula grandiflora, "the Kerry violet", an insectivorous plant found in boggy mountain reaches.

▼ Pinguicula grandiflora, planda feithiditeach a fhásann sa sliabh.

▼ La grassette Pinguicula grandiflora, plante carnivore découverte dans les étendues tourbeuses des collines.

▼ Pinguicula grandiflora, das "Kerry-Veilchen", eine insektenfressende Pflanze, die in sumpfigen Berggegenden wächst.

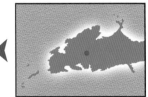
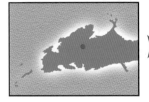

▶ The waterfall below Pedlar's lake on the Conor Pass road, with Mount Brandon in the background.

▶ Eas taobh thíos de Loch an Pheidléara ar bhóthar na Conarach, agus radharc ar Chnoc Bhréanainn laistiar.

▶ Cascade en amont du lac Pedlar, sur la route menant au col de Conor. A l'arrière plan, le mont Brandon.

▶ Der Wasserfall unter Pedlar's Lake am Conor-Pass, mit Mount Brandon im Hintergrund.

▼ Rahinnane Castle, Ventry. There are many such castles in the peninsula, most of which were built in the sixteenth century and destroyed by the Cromwellian army. This castle has been built within an earlier ringfort.

▼ Caisleán Ráthanáin, Fionntrá. Tá caisleáin dá leithéid seo flúirseach go leor timpeall na leithinise. Tógadh a bhformhór sa 16ú haois agus leag arm Chromail iad. Tá caisleán Ráthanáin tógtha i lár leasa.

▼ Château de Rahinnane à Ventry. La péninsule possède de nombreux châteaux de ce type, édifiés pour la plupart au 16eme siècle puis détruits par l'armée de Cromwell. Ce château fut construit au sein de ce qui était alors une ancienne forteresse.

▼ Rahinnane Castle, Ventry. Es gibt viele solcher Burgen auf der Halbinsel, von denen die meisten im 16. Jahrhundert erbaut und später von der Armee Cromwells zerstört wurden. Die Burg wurde innerhalb eines früheren Ringforts errichtet.

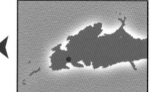

▶ Dunbeg promontory fort at Fahan. There are many such Iron Age coastal promontory forts on the peninsula, and Dunbeg is unusual for the structures that have survived: its fosses and banks, dry-stone rampart and large beehive hut, or *clochán*.

▶ An Dún Beag i bhFán. Tá a leithéidí seo flúirseach go leor ar fuaid na leithinise, ach tá an ceann seo neamhghnáthach ó thaobh go maireann an clochán agus na bunstruchtúir.

▶ Promontoire du fort de Dunbeg, à Fahan. La péninsule compte un nombre important de forteresses datant de l'âge de fer. Les fondations de celle de Dunberg ont résisté à l'érosion du temps: fossés et talus, remparts et huttes rondes ou *clochán* (clocher).

▶ Das Küstenfort von Dunbeg bei Fahan. Es gibt viele Beispiele solcher Steinforts aus der Eisenzeit auf der Halbinsel; ungewöhnlich an Dunbeg sind die Konstruktionen, die bis heute erhalten geblieben sind: Aussengräben und irdene Schutzwälle, Steinwälle, ohne Mörtel errichtet, und eine grosse Bienenkorbhütte (*clochán*).

▼ Two sisters pay the round at St John the Baptist's Well, near Minard Castle, on the patron day.

▼ Beirt deirféar ag déanamh turas na Croise ag tobar Naomh Eoin Baiste lámh le Caisleán na Min Airde.

▼ Deux sœurs «paient la tournée» à la fontaine saint Jean-Baptiste, près du château de Minard, le jour de la saint.

▼ Zwei Schwestern beten am Brunnen des Täufers Johannes, in der Nähe von Minard Castle, am Namenstag des Heiligen.

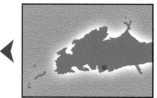
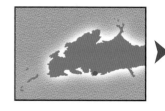

▶ Minard Castle, built in the sixteenth century, a former stronghold of the Knight of Kerry; in 1650 it was bombarded by the Cromwellian army and all its defenders were killed.

▶ Caisleán na Min Airde. Is le Ridire Chiarraí an caisleán seo a tógadh sa 16ú haois. D'ionsaigh arm Chromail é sa bhliain 1650 agus maraíodh na cosantóirí ar fad.

▶ Le château de Minard, édifié au 16ème siècle, est une ancienne forteresse du bras droit du Chevalier de Kerry. Il fut détruit lors d'une attaque orchestrée par Cromwell où tous ses habitants périrent.

▶ Minard Castle, erbaut im 16. Jahrhundert, früher die Hochburg der Ritter von Kerry; 1650 wurde sie von der Armee Cromwells bombardiert, wobei alle ihrer Verteidiger ums Leben kamen.

▼ Sheep beside Anascaul lake.

▼ Caoirigh le hais Loch an Scáil.

▼ Moutons en bordure du lac Anascaul.

▼ Schafe am See von Anascaul.

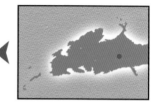

▶ Anascaul lake: From the spurs above it, the hero Cúchulainn and a giant hurled boulders at each other.

▶ Loch an Scáil. Ar na speiríní os cionn na locha seo a bhí an fathach agus Cúchulainn ag crústach a chéile le carraigeacha.

▶ Lac Anascaul, au-dessus duquel Cúchulainn et le géant s'affrontèrent en s'envoyant des blocs rocheux.

▶ Der See von Anascaul: Von den Felsvorsprüngen oberhalb des Sees bekämpften Cúchulainn und ein Riese sich gegenseitig mit Felsbrocken.

▼ Doonsheane, the fort of the fairies; one of many coastal promontory forts associated with the Iron Age.

▼ Dún Sidhean. Baineann an lios seo le Ré an Iarrainn.

▼ Doonsheane, le château des fées: un des nombreux promontoires de pierre surplombant la mer et datant de l'âge de fer.

▼ Dunsheane, das Feenfort, eines von vielen Küstenforts, die der Eisenzeit zugerechnet werden.

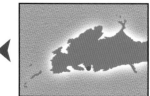

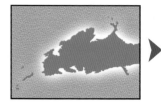

▶ The yellow iris, or flag grows profusely in roadside ditches and in marshes and wet fields.

▶ Fásann an bláth seo, an liostram buí, go forleathan sna goirt fhliucha agus i ndígeacha na mbóithre.

▶ L'iris des marais ou fleur de lis, pousse à profusion dans les fossés bordant les routes, les chemins de traverse, les champs humides et les marécages.

▶ Die gelbe Schwertlilie wächst in Hülle und Fülle in Strassengräben, Sümpfen und auf Feuchtwiesen.

▼ A stormy autumn day at Lough Gill, as rainclouds from the west break over Mount Brandon.

▼ Lá stoirmiúil geimhridh ar Loch Gile agus báisteach ar Chnoc Bhréanainn.

▼ Journée d'automne orageuse à Lough Gill: des nuages menaçants, provenant de l'ouest et chargés de pluie s'abattent sur le mont Brandon.

▼ Ein stürmischer Herbsttag am Lough Gill während eines Wolkenbruches über Mount Brandon.

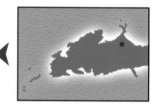

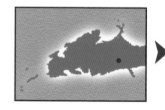

▶ View north towards Anascaul lake.

▶ Radharc ar Loch an Scáil.

▶ Vue en direction du nord vers le lac Anascaul.

▶ Blick nach Norden in Richtung des Sees von Anascaul.

▼ Boat at Trabeg, with the Strickeen mountain behind.

▼ Bád ar an dTráigh Bheag, agus radharc ar Starraicín laistiar.

▼ Bateau à Trabeg avec à l'arrière plan la montagne Strickeen.

▼ Boot in Trabeg, mit der Bergspitze Strickeen im Hintergrund.

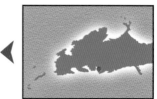

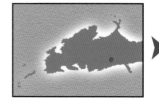

▶ The river at Anascaul, the home village of explorer Tom Crean and sculptor Jerome Connor.

▶ Abhainn an Scáil as ar ainmníodh an baile inar saolaíodh an taiscéalaí Tom Crean agus an dealbhóir Jerome Connor.

▶ Rivière Anascaul qui porte le nom du village natal de l'explorateur Tom Crean et du sculpteur Jérôme Connor.

▶ Der Fluss in Anascaul, dem Heimatort des Arktikforschers Tom Crean und des Bildhauers Jerome Connor.

▼ Lough Slat in Glanteenassig, the forested valleys of the waterfall.

▼ Loch Slat i nGleannta an Easaigh.

▼ Lough Slat à Glanteenassig, vallées boisées bordant la cascade.

▼ Lough Slat in Glanteenassig, die bewaldeten Täler des Wasserfalles.

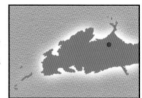
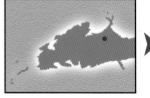

▶ View from the bridge in Glanteenassig.

▶ Radharc ó dhroichead Ghleannta an Easaigh.

▶ Vue du pont de Glanteenassig.

▶ Blick von der Brücke in Glanteenassig.

A naomhog team at Brandon. The naomhog is the tarred canvas craft which is called a curragh in other parts of Ireland; once used in great numbers for fishing, they are now used for sport, and the peninsula boasts several naomhog regattas during the summer.

Criú naomhóige i mBréanainn. "Curach" a ghlaotar ar an mbáidín beag seo in áiteanna eile, ach "naomhóga" a ghlaotar orthu anseo. Go dtí le déanaí is chun iascaireachta a d'úsáidtí iad, ach is chun spóirt is mó a úsáidtear anois iad, go háirithe ag ráiseanna ar nós regatta an Daingin agus a leithéidí eile ar fuaid na leithinise.

Equipage d'un Naomhog à Brandon. Le Naomhog est une embarcation faite de toile ou de peau imperméabilisée au bitume et appelée "curragh" (coracle) dans les autres régions d'Irlande; jadis principalement utilisé pour la pêche, sa vocation est maintenant sportive. La péninsule est particulièrement fière d'accueillir les nombreuses régates qui s'y déroulent en été.

Eine 'naomhog' - Rudermannschaft in Brandon. Ein naomhog ist ein geteertes, leinenbespanntes Boot, das in anderen Landstrichen Irlands als 'curragh' bekannt ist; es wurde früher in grossen Mengen zum Fischfang benutzt, dient heute aber überwiegend als Sportboot in den zahlreichen Ruderregatten während der Sommermonate.

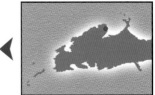

Watching the naomhog racing at Brandon.

Ag féachaint ar ráiseanna naomhóg i mBréanainn.

Spectacle offert par une course de coracles à Brandon.

Zuschauer bei der Ruderregatta in Brandon.

▼ Roadside flowers near Cloghane.

▼ Bláthanna ag fás ar thaobh an bhóthair sa Chlochán.

▼ Fleurs de talus à proximité de Cloghane.

▼ Blumen am Strassenrand bei Cloghane.

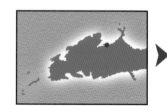

▶ Fermoyle

▶ Formaoil

▶ Fermoyle

▶ Fermoyle

▼ Children playing in a stream, Ballintlea, Ventry.

▼ Leanaí ag seó i sruthán beag i mBaile an tSléibhe, Fionntrá.

▼ Enfants jouant dans un ruisseau, Ballintlea, Ventry.

▼ Spielende Kinder in einem Bach, Ballintlea, Ventry.

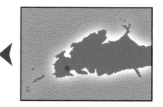

▶ Ogham stones at Páirc na Fola (field of blood), Lispole.

▶ Clocha oghaim ag Páirc na Fola, Lios Póil.

▶ Pierres d'Ogham à Pairc na Fola, Lispole.

▶ Ogham-Steine auf Pairc na Fola (Blutfeld), Lispole.

▼ Mount Brandon in mid-winter.

▼ Cnoc Bhréanainn i lár an gheimhridh.

▼ Mont Brandon au cœur de l'hiver.

▼ Mount Brandon im Winter.

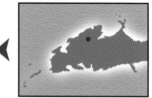

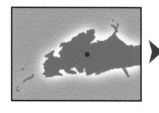

▶ View south from the Conor Pass road.

▶ Ag féachaint ó dheas ó Bhóthar na Conarach.

▶ Vue en direction du sud depuis la route menant au Conor Pass.

▶ Blick Richtung Süden vom Conor-Pass.

▼ Low cloud at dawn at Inch strand.

▼ Inch strand: nuage bas à l'aube.

▼ Go moch ar maidin ar thráigh Inse.

▼ Tiefhängende Wolken bei Tagesanbruch am Strand von Inch.

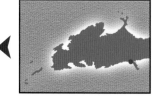

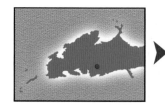

▶ Gallán at An Ghráig, Lispole.

▶ Gallán (menhir) à An Ghráig, Lispole.

▶ Gallán ar an nGráig, Lios Póil.

▶ Gallán (stehender Stein) in An Ghráig, Lispole.

▼ The route of the Dingle Way rises from the Finglas river at Camp.

▼ Tosnaíonn Slí Chorca Dhuibhne ag abhainn Fionnghlaise ar an gCam.

▼ La route de Dingle Way s'élevant au-dessus de la rivière Finglas de Camp.

▼ Der Dingle Way-Wanderweg führt hinter dem Fluss Finglas bei Camp bergauf.

▶ The old road pursues a ruler-straight line through the village of Anascaul.

▶ An sean-bhóthar ag dul cruinn díreach trí Abhainn an Scáil.

▶ La vieille route de Dingle Way traverse de part en part le village d'Anascaul.

▶ Die alte Strasse führt schnurgerade durch Anascaul.

▼ Milking time at Annagap, near Anascaul.

▼ Na ba á gcrú in Áth na gCeap, in aice le hAbhainn an Scáil.

▼ Heure de la traite à Annagap, près d'Anascaul.

▼ Melkzeit in Annagap, bei Anascaul.

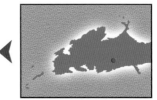

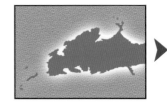

▶ Foxgloves flourish in the ditches.

▶ Fásann méaracáin dhearga go flúirseach ar na clathacha.

▶ Digitales fleurissant dans les fossés.

▶ Blühende Fingerhüte in den Gräben.

▼ A field of yellow iris near the village of Castlegregory.

▼ Liostram buí ag fás i ngort i gCaisleán an Ghriaire.

▼ Champ d'iris des marais près du village de Castlegregory.

▼ Ein Feld blühender Schwertlilien in der Nähe von Castlegregory.

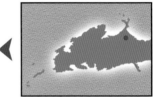

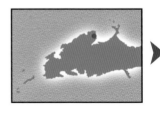

▶ Young dancers, Brandon quay.

▶ Rinceoirí óga ar ché Bhréanainn.

▶ Jeunes danseurs sur la jetée de Brandon.

▶ Junge Volkstänzer, am Pier von Brandon.

▼ In the bog, Owenmore valley.

▼ Ar an bportach i nGleann na hAbhann Móire.

▼ Au milieu des tourbières, la vallée d'Owenmore.

▼ Auf dem Hochmoor, das Owenmore-Tal.

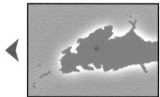

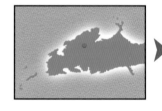

▶ Mount Brandon and the Owenmore valley on a fine winter's day.

▶ Lá breá geimhridh ar Chnoc Bhréanainn agus i nGleann na hAbhann Móire.

▶ Le mont Brandon et la vallée d'Owenmore par une belle journée d'hiver.

▶ Mount Brandon und das Owenmore-Tal an einem schönen Wintertag.

▼ Naomhóg and Mount Brandon.

▼ Naomhóg agus Cnoc Bhréanainn.

▼ Coracles et le mont Brandon.

▼ Naomhóg und Mount Brandon.

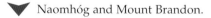

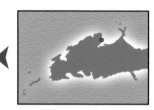

▶ Mount Brandon from the air.

▶ Cnoc Bhréanainn ón aer.

▶ Vue aérienne du mont Brandon.

▶ Mount Brandon aus der Luft gesehen.

▼ Cloghane

▼ An Clochán

▼ Cloghane

▼ Cloghane

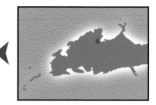

▶ Loosestrife and montbretia, two of the common roadside plants.

▶ Seo dhá phlanda atá flúirseach go maith anseo, liostram dearg agus eireaball caitín.

▶ La Lysamaque ou herbe aux écus et la Montbretia, deux favorites des fossés.

▶ Blut-Weiderich und Montbretie, zwei der häufigsten Pflanzen am Strassenrand.

Naomhógs at rest; the tarred-canvas canoes are sometimes fitted with outboard engines, and a few are still used as working craft, while many are used for racing.

Naomhóga ar stáitsí.

Coracles amarrés; un moteur équipe parfois ces embarcations de toile enduite. Bien que quelques uns servent encore à la pêche, ils sont aujourd'hui majoritairement utilisés dans les courses de vitesse.

Naomhógs auf ihren Ständen. Die leinenbespannten Boote sind manchmal mit einem Aussenbordmotor ausgerüstet, und einige werden immer noch zum Fischfang benutzt, während die meisten heutzutage in Ruderregatten zum Einsatz kommen.

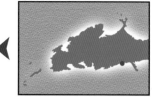

Blennerville windmill as a violent rainstorm approaches.

An muileann gaoithe i gCathair Uí Mhóráin is scrabha báistí ag teacht.

Moulin à vent de Blennerville: un violent orage menace.

Die Windmühle in Blennerville beim Anzug eines Unwetters.

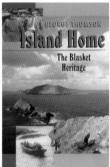

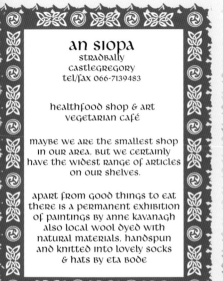

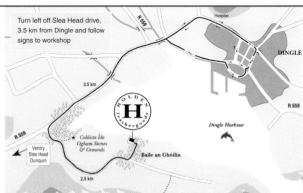
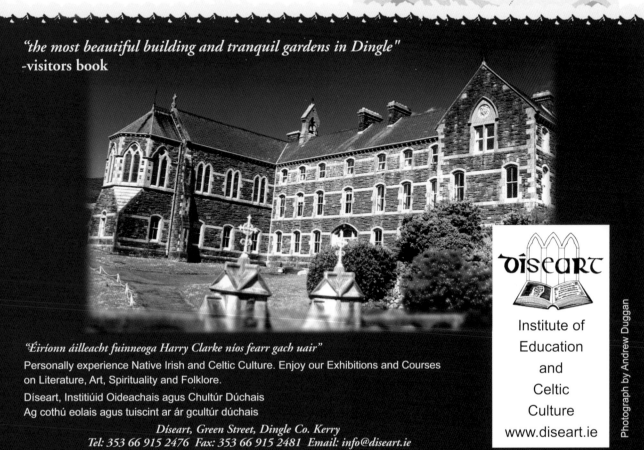

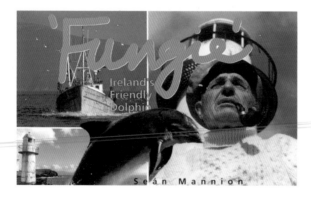
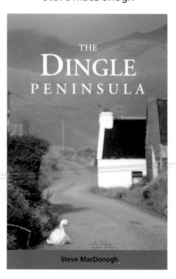